AFFILIATE MARKETING 101.

HOW TO MAKE MONEY FROM HOME WITH AFFILIATE MARKETING.

Author: John Shaw.

Copyright: 2018

CONTENTS

How To Make Money From Home With Affiliate Marketing. 1
Introduction. 3
What Is Affiliate Marketing? 4
An Overview. 4
Affiliate Marketing. 11
Where To Start? 11
Finding Your Niche. 13
Show Me The Money! 16
How To Find The Best Affiliate Partners. 18
A Website Or A Blog? 20
Building Your Business. 23
Develop A Rapport. 24
Find Quality Products. 25
Establish Your Presence. 26
Get Some Traffic! 28
Conclusion. 35

My Recommended Resources.

INTRODUCTION.

I'd written about 15 pages of this little book when I sat down and thought "why am I bothering? There are 100s of books about affiliate marketing, many of them much more informative than this, why would anyone want this book?"
And then I remembered, when I first started affiliate marketing back in 2006 there was very little information that I could get free that would tell me the whole story.
All would offer some information and then ask for a subscription or try to sell an expensive course for me to get the real info that I needed.
It was really frustrating then and nothing much has changed.
You'll still get enough info to whet your appetite and then you'll be asked to part with sometimes quite large amounts of cash to learn how to make the whole thing work.
Not here.
There's no upsell, no course to buy, no membership to join, with this little book you get everything you need to know to get started on what may be the most exciting, and financially rewarding journey of your life.
Enjoy,
John.

WHAT IS AFFILIATE MARKETING?

An Overview.

This is probably a really good place to start a book about Affiliate Marketing.
Most people who are looking to make some money from home via the internet will have heard the term, many will know what it is and how it works but some will not so here is the best definition I have found:
Affiliate Marketing is: a marketing arrangement by which an online retailer pays commission to an external website for traffic or sales generated from its referrals.
Quite simple really, someone puts up a website or a blog and places affiliate links on that site and whenever that link is activated by a website visitor the affiliate marketer is paid a commission.
As I said, quite simple really, except, well, it's not quite that simple.
If you've been around for any more than a day or two you've seen a good number of (outrageous) claims that by following this plan or by doing it this or that way you can be up and running with your website and making generous amounts of cash by this time next week.
I have to tell you that is just baloney!
You will also have heard that most affiliate marketers are making more money than they know what to do with.
Many will put "screenshots" of their "bank deposits" on their sites to show you just how successful they've become just from following the formula or the plan.
It's really easy to mock up a "bank statement" and it proves nothing, don't be taken in by it.
To be honest, many of these apparently successful affiliate marketers are much better at selling their story than they are at making affiliate commissions, almost all are better at communicating their easy way to riches than I am at telling you that while it is definitely possible it isn't all that easy.
Who you decide to believe is, of course, up to you, you can take the information here or leave it, your choice, all I will say is it works for me.
I will tell you now that there are affiliate links on some of these pages and should you choose to

follow those links I may be compensated in some way, that's affiliate marketing.

The reality regarding affiliate marketing is that there are a few who have made it big, some have even made it very big, there are many more who make a good living or at least they make enough to satisfy their goals but, sadly, the majority barely make enough money to cover their costs.

The question that you must ask yourself before embarking on this (potentially) life changing journey isn't whether or not affiliate marketing is a feasible income option, it obviously is, but whether or not affiliate marketing is feasible for you.

Only you can decide that.

But to help, here are some things to consider before you commit.

On the positive side:
- There is little or no cost to get started, any costs you do incur should only be related to your chosen marketing method/s as any good affiliate programme will be free to join, if it isn't, investigate it thoroughly before you pay to join.
- There is no need for you to create your own product or service, you'll be selling other people's goods.
- There is no stock for you to hold or ship, that will all be done for you by your affiliate merchant.
- Likewise you shouldn't have to worry about returns or refunds, that is your merchant's problem.
- You can work from anywhere you have an internet connection and at whatever time of day suits you best.
- You have the potential to build a business that offers you a true passive income, the holy grail if you will.
- You can attach your affiliate business to almost any other web based endeavour you may already have. If you blog, for example, you can sell your affiliate goods and services via your blog etc..

On the negative side there are some challenges you'll have to overcome before you'll make any decent money from affiliate marketing, some of these are:
- Affiliate marketing, no matter how you do it, is unlikely to make you a decent income in the short term, it's a process you'll need to work at and build.
- You'll need to find ways to generate traffic to your affiliate links, and it needs to be relevant traffic. Obviously the more traffic you get from people who may be interested in your offering the more you'll sell and the more money you'll make.
- There are plenty of crooks around and the internet is no different, there will always be people, and organisations, who will rip you off if given the opportunity. Some merchants will try to short change you by hacking your traffic, the good news here is there are ways to prevent this and masking your URL will help.
- Your credibility is your lifeblood as far as your clients are concerned, choose to work with only reputable and reliable merchants, a bad affiliate connection can so easily ruin it. Guard your credibility as though your life depends on it, your business certainly does.
- You have control over your side of your business but you have no control over how your merchants act. Many an affiliate business has been shut down by, for example, their chosen merchants ceasing to trade.
- There are some less reputable merchants who have been guilty of not honouring their side of the agreement and just refusing payment to their affiliates.
- Your customers actually don't belong to you they "belong" to the merchant whose goods you're promoting. In most cases you have no information regarding who makes a purchase, this changes, of course, if you can get them to sign up to your regular newsletter.

Affiliate marketing is almost the ideal home business, it's easy and inexpensive to get started and you can do it while you're still working your J.O.B. but it does require some knowledge, some planning, proper commitment and a good deal of persistence.

The best way to approach this is as though you are working for a boss, you have set hours, it doesn't matter when they are but you need to commit to so many hours each and every day.

For me it's very early in the morning, I sit with a cup of coffee before the rest of the house has started moving and I do what I need to do before anything else, I find that if I leave it until later there's always something else more pressing that needs to be done.

You'll soon find out what suits you best if you don't know already.

You'll need to source some products or services to promote.

It's important here that you look for quality affiliate products that interest you, there's very little that's worse that trying to promote something you have little or no interest in, I know , I've been there and done that a number of times.

It's very easy to get blinded by the sometimes insane amounts of money some affiliate programmes are offering, as many will tell you it's just as easy to sell something that's worth $1000 as it is to sell something that's only worth $10 but that doesn't apply if you have no interest in the product.

Your customers will be able to tell that you aren't really convinced about it's worth, don't ask me how they know I can't tell you, but know they will.

Do your due diligence before you sign up to an affiliate programme, make sure you understand your relationship with your merchants, what they do and do not allow when it comes to your own marketing efforts and the terms under which you'll get paid.

Some merchants will pay you each month regardless of how much money you've made but most will have a payment threshold you must reach before they'll send you money.

Once you've decided on a product or programme it's a good idea to start a blog or website about your particular niche or if you already have a web presence in place then ensure that you fit your affiliate business in line with that as you'll probably have a following already in place.

It's of little use for you to promote the sale of children's clothing if you operate a blog or website about Harley Davidson motorcycles.

Once again:

It is important that you disclose your affiliate relationships very early on and on every page of your site or blog, it's illegal, especially in the USA to place affiliate links without declaring your relationship to the merchants whose goods or services you're promoting.

You will have noticed that I have placed a statement very early in this little book stating that there are affiliate links in place throughout this publication, you can't be too careful regarding this, as Nike says, "Just Do It!"

When you're placing your ads for your affiliate products or services be careful not to overdo it and load up ads on your pages or in your newsletter.

It's worth noting that while flashy image ads look good and attract attention it's the "in content" affiliate links that get most of the clicks.

A few well placed and relevant affiliate links sprinkled through your content has proved to be the most profitable way to get the click that you're after.

Writing product reviews is a good way to get your business but if you write a review or an article about a particular product or service it's important that those reading your article are informed regarding your relationship with the provider of that product or service.

This ensures you retain transparency and trust with your readers, but also, it's required by the FTC's endorsement rules and not to do so will leave you liable for some quite hefty financial penalties.

NOW once you've got your business up and running you have to get traffic.

But all traffic isn't equal.

Once again, 10,000 visitors from people who ride Harleys is no good if your blog is about pre-school tuckshops.

Relevance is the key, your traffic must be relevant to the offers you're promoting, it's just common sense.

A word of caution here, don't buy traffic, at best it's useless and it can cost you a lot of money and if you add those bought names to your email list you stand a very good chance of being pinged as being a spammer.

You'll need to market your on-line presence by whatever means you can without relying on any one source regardless of how good it seems and you need to own your marketing efforts so that you can't be sidelined by what someone else does.

Spread your effort between as many different traffic sources as you can find but make sure you don't spread yourself too thin, that will defeat the purpose.

It's important to identify your audience or your potential audience and engage them in places where they currently have a presence.

Again, to use that silly example, you wouldn't join a forum frequented by new moms if you want to engage Harley riders.

Find some decent forums which offer you a chance to establish relationships with potential clients and when you do don't fall into the trap of only pitching your affiliate offers or of thinking that everyone will want to buy what you're selling.

Forums are generally places where people exchange ideas, if you become involved with the community before you make your pitch you'll stand a much better chance of being heard at some later stage, especially if you can then answer a question or provide a solution to someone's problem your stocks will go up and so will your sales.

It's the same deal with social media.

It's called social media for a reason so don't overlook the "social" part and you get a much better response.

"What about email" I hear you say, many if not all successful affiliate marketers have a good email list.

You will probably have heard the phrase "the money's in the list" and it's quite true.

The bigger email list you have the more people you have to send your offering to but it has to be a good, relevant list.
As I've said above about traffic, an email list that you've purchased will cause you many more problems than it will solve.
Apart from the fact that your bought email list will probably have a great percentage of addresses which don't exist anymore, when you send to those that are still open you'll certainly be accused of spamming and that can kill your business almost before you get it started.
So how do you get a good, relevant email list?
There's a very good article at:
https://bit.ly/2LsUdPn which will give you the basics about how to build an email list from scratch but put very (very) simply it amounts to offering something of value in exchange for an email address.
If someone wants to receive your giveaway (or whatever your offer is) they must first ask for it and give you their email address in exchange.
Of course it's a little more complicated than that so follow the link and read the article to learn more.
The most successful affiliate marketers use email in their affiliate marketing so don't put this off.
Email marketing can increase your affiliate profits significantly.
Moving on from basic email marketing you can utilise what's called a "funnel system" to add more offers to your prospects.
Generate a lead page to collect email addresses and feed those addresses into your funnel which, in turn, will send them to your offer or offers.
Then in your email system, you can offer more great free content and more affiliate offers.
Most successful affiliate marketers will tell you that the best prospects are those who have already purchased from you, if you start with something which is relatively inexpensive those who purchase it will be much more likely to buy a more expensive item at a later date.
They have already had a positive experience with you so are much less reluctant to part with their money a second, or third, or fourth time.

Just one more thing before I get into the nitty gritty, those who study these things tell us that in the U.S alone the market spend via affiliate marketing will be almost $7 billion by 2020, I'm sure we would all like perhaps just a small piece of that pie, wouldn't you agree?

So if you're still interested after reading that let's get started.

AFFILIATE MARKETING.
Where To Start?

Most will tell you that you should first choose the product/s or service/s which you'd like to promote and build your business from there.
They'll tell you to pick high value products which will make you good dollars on every sale or alternatively pick small value items that you can sell a lot of, a bit like the local car dealer against your local grocery store.
That's not bad advice.
But before you go looking for your niche the better route is to first look for your niche audience.
Why?
Well products change, they come and go and what's popular today may just be yesterday's favourite come tomorrow but the people who bought the product or service yesterday will still be there tomorrow and they'll still be looking for something to scratch their itch.
If you take time to choose your niche audience and fully understand their needs then finding products or services to satisfy those needs becomes a much easier task.

When you understand your prospective clients/customers you will then be able to easily find products and services to satisfy their needs. Not only that but as one product goes out of fashion you'll easily find others to replace it, you'll have an almost never ending supply of customers with needs or desires and a bottomless pot of products to offer them.

It just makes too much sense not to do it this way. When I started affiliate marketing in 2006 I did it the "wrong" way round and struggled to make any decent money, today I'm a little wiser and now make all I need from the various passive income streams I've since created by concentrating on the needs of my audience rather than on the products I like to promote.

What is also important here is finding a profitable niche, one that you can invest yourself in, and sticking to it.

A big mistake which is made by almost all new affiliate marketers, and it's a mistake I've made myself, is not concentrating on just one, or possibly two profitable niches.

It's very tempting to follow this or that "new" trend, to try and find "the next big thing" but it doesn't work.

That said, finding a niche that has a receptive audience and one that will work for you out of the many thousands, yes thousands of niches available to you, sometimes isn't easy and some of the advice you'll read about niche marketing isn't really all that good.

"It's too competitive" is one that's often bandied about, "there isn't a market for that", "the big players have it all sewn up", there's always someone trying to de-rail you when the truth is that there are untold millions of internet users and a significant percentage of those will be looking for whatever it is you're marketing regardless of how "way out" it may appear, all you have to do is find them and place your offer in front of them in an appealing way.

(An example of this, I did a Google search for the term "put a sock in a toaster", who on earth would search for a term like that? Only 16,000,000 people,

yes that's 16 million searches for that term so, for me, that proves that someone, somewhere will be searching for anything you want to promote).
SO how do you find a niche that is a good fit for your future business?

Finding Your Niche.

When you're looking to find your own profitable niche it's as well to consider this:
There are some niches that will always be popular and profitable, these are known as "evergreen" niches, for obvious reasons.
An evergreen niche is a niche with permanent and ongoing appeal.
It doesn't rely on seasonal trends or gimmicks to attract customers because it sells products or services that people inherently need or desire and they're desirable because they make money year after year.
Evergreen niches not only make money year after year, they do not need aggressive marketing they represent lower investment risk and they offer a potential for long-term profit.
So how do you decide if your niche is an evergreen niche?
Just ask yourself the following questions:
Does it address an intrinsic human problem or interest, does its appeal have an expiration date and is it conducive to growth and profit?
If the answer to these questions is "yes" then you probably have an evergreen niche.
It's generally accepted that there are 6 or 7 niches which genuinely fall into the category of "evergreen".

These are:
Relationships and dating.
Health.
Mental health.
Weight loss.
Gaming.
Sports and hobbies.
Technology.

All of that said you don't have to work in one of these markets, your affiliate business is about you after all, but you might want to consider how you may perhaps incorporate some of these ideas into your own affiliate marketing programme.

NOW, there are almost as many ways to find a niche as there are niches but I prefer to use the KISS principle, (if you don't know KISS is an acronym for Keep It Simple Stupid!)

In my mind there are just four easy steps to finding a profitable niche for your business.

1. Brainstorm an audience.

You can do this in a number of ways.
You can choose your prospective audience from the demographic that you belong to yourself.
You already know what you, and therefore they, like, what they need or need to know.

2. Identify the problems your niche audience has.

Here you work in reverse, pick a subject that interests you or satisfies a need that you have and apply it to your audience, after all, they think like you and they have, more or less, the same desires and needs as you have.

Take this a step further and do a little research into the challenges they face, what causes them the most pain, what their desires and aspirations are. You can do this online by visiting some of the multitude of niche forums, popular niche blogs (which will eventually become your competition) and "how to" websites to find your answers.

3. Pick out the most profitable problems.

Remember here that not all problems are created equal, some are bigger than others and some will be harder to overcome but with some digging you'll find those situations which your audience will be prepared to pay to solve and those which are really just nuisance value.

Make a list of all the problems or unanswered queries you find and then arrange them in order of your perceived profitability.
This should give you an idea of the solutions or answers your potential clients would be most likely to pay to solve.

4. Develop a deep understanding of that/those problems.

It isn't enough to know that overweight people are looking for a weight loss solution, you must understand where their weight comes from, what they will likely have already tried and why it didn't work, you will need to get into their heads and understand how frustrating it is and how downright unhappy it makes them.

When you can start to think like your prospect and see the problems from his or her perspective then you've got a good shot at making your niche work for you.

Here's a quote (more or less) from a man named Adam Chandler:
"Everyone has at least one passion on which they will gleefully spend insane amounts of money." (ask any golfer or fisherman).
As an affiliate marketer all you have to do is find the passion and put your offering in front of the passionate and you'll get your share of those insane amounts of money.
Believe it, it's true!

Talking about money, how do you get paid as an affiliate marketer?

Read on!

Show Me The Money!

There are several different models used by various merchants when it comes to paying affiliate commissions and you should understand these before you start to promote your offerings to your prospects because the commissions you earn relate directly to whichever model your chosen merchant/s use.

In the simplest terms commission payments are based either on a Cost Per Sale or a Cost Per Action basis.

Cost Per Sale (CPS), also referred to as Pay Per Sale (PPS), is the model used by many marketers of high profit items as it is, for them, very low risk. If their affiliate makes a sale and that sale is finalised and payed for, then, and only then, will they send the payment to the referring affiliate.

It's a win/win for the merchant, if there is no sale they pay no commission but they still get the (free) advertising generated by the affiliate.

On top of that they will often get a prospects email address so they follow up without involving the affiliate.

For the affiliate it can mean that you put in a lot of work which is essentially unrewarded.

On the positive side CPS payout commissions are generally much higher than those offered in the Cost Per Action model with some merchants offering commissions as high as 80%.

I even know of one merchant who pays 100% of the initial sale and he makes his money on the "backend" or follow-up sales.

Cost Per Action (CPA) is a model in which the affiliate gets paid when a prospect he/she sends to a merchant takes a specific action.

This may be as simple as clicking a link, submitting a form, signing up for something, registering, opting in or even just showing an impression on a website or mailer.

Since the payment of a commission here is not dependant on a sale happening the commissions are generally considerably lower than that in the CPS model.

This doesn't mean that you should ignore the CPA model, if you have a good relationship with your prospect base and can generate lots of traffic to your website or mailer then you can make good money here without the need to convince anyone to buy anything.

The hotel industry makes good use of this model and I myself make commissions from a top line hotel aggregator just being paid a measly 15 to 75 cents per click.

If that's the kind of business that floats your boat go for it, you can still earn a very good income from CPA.

Of course you can always do as I do and combine the two, have some merchants who pay you per click and some who pay per sale, you make money either way.

Whichever model you decide to adopt it is very important to align yourself with a merchant or merchants who are trustworthy, merchants who you feel comfortable will pay you your commissions at the right rate and on time.

How do you find good, trustworthy partners?
That comes next!

How To Find The Best Affiliate Partners.

Before you decide to become an affiliate marketer you're faced with a number of possibilities regarding the direction of your business and with the number of options available to you.

You could, for example, promote and market your own products, you could employ a drop shipping programme, you could start a membership site and so on.
The fact that you've decided to embark, at least initially, on the affiliate business model gives you a very do-able opportunity to make money, be it a little extra or a whole lot more, you can work your business part-time, which is where most of us start, or you could just jump in "boots and all" and go for broke.
However you decide to start it will be very, no extremely deflating if you make that first commission cheque only to find that your chosen merchant has found a way they can avoid paying you and it won't matter whether it's hundreds of dollars or just a few cents, it will leave you feeling gutted.
I've been there and it isn't nice at all.
Worse than that is when you realise that there really is nothing you can do about it.
If a shop keeper did it to you you'd go to the authorities and you'd have some recourse but that isn't going to work here.
The answer is to make very sure that those you're in business with are reputable and trustworthy but how do you do that?
The answer to that question may seem obvious but it bears stating here, you trust the merchants that most others trust.
There are any number of affiliate merchants who do, and will always do, the right thing, merchants like Amazon and eBay can't afford to have their reputation sullied by engaging in dodgy practises and there are also programmes like Clickbank and Commission Junction (CJ) who act as intermediaries between merchants and affiliates to ensure that everything is done in a fair and businesslike manner.
Just as with any other business investment, and you will be investing your time if not your money, do your due diligence before you sign up.
A little later I've written a section entitled "Resources" where I'll be giving you a few names of programmes you can trust to do the right thing, just

be aware, if you click on the links I may be compensated in some way.
But first ……

A Website Or A Blog?

One thing you'll need when you start your affiliate marketing business is a web presence and you really only have two choices, a website or a blog.
What's the difference you may ask, read on.
A Blog.
"Blog" is a shortened version of "weblog" and it is what the name says it is, it's a web log or a chronological listing of blog posts.
When someone visits your blog page they find themselves reading the latest information you've placed there followed by the previous post and so on, in chronological order, newest to oldest.
It's easy to start a blog and you can do it without any financial investment at all.
There are platforms like WordPress and Blogger which will allow you to start your blog for free, they will also provide you with a good choice of

templates for your blog and some help when you need it.
You can investigate WordPress here:
You can investigate Blogger here:
To be relevant, and to attract the attention of the likes of Google, a blog needs to be updated on a reasonably regular basis or the information on it will possibly be viewed as stale and out of date and potential visitors may dismiss it.
That said, the information you publish on your blog needs to be good and original, as with all things in life you won't be able to convert crap into gold or the proverbial pigs ear into a silk purse.
If you can update your blog at least weekly with good, original content then you may do well with a blog, it is, however, a regular commitment if you wish to make it a success.
To see a few examples of successful blogs visit these sites:
Techcrunch, Mashable, Cnet, ShoutMeLoud, LifeHacker, Gizmodo, Kotaku, etc. and the list goes on.
A blog also generally will include an option whereby you can invite your readers to participate in the communication and leave behind their comments and will also allow for "Really Simple Syndication" (RSS) via feed readers like Feedly etc..
A website.
A website can be almost anything that's presented on the internet in one or other of the "internet languages" such as HTML/CSS or Java/Javascript/Python/Php, etc.
"I don't know any of that" you say.
Fear not, these days you don't have to.
But before I get into that, what actually constitutes "a website"?
Well, for our purposes a website can have 1 page, an email sign up page for example, or it can have several hundreds or thousands of pages each about a different aspect of the site's particular subject or niche.
As an example I have a website which has over 800 pages about Australia and I also have a site with just 1 page which invites visitors to subscribe to my newsletter.

A website generally has a homepage which is the first, or introduction, page and it will have a navigation system to enable visitors to find other pages which they might be interested in.
These might include an "about this site" page, a "contact" page, a "frequently asked questions" page that readers can browse to get more information and so on.
A website might also have a blog attached to it where the owners post regularly updated information. To use one of my own sites again as an example, my travel site has a blog attached which regularly informs my visitors of the latest cruise deals on offer from various Australian ports as well as special hotel deals etc..
If you're relatively new to all of this, and I assume you are or you wouldn't be reading this little book, there are a number of ways you can start a website just as there are with a blog however there are some disadvantages with a free website not the least of these is not having your own domain name.
When you use a free site the name that appears in the address bar will always indicate that the site is free and that doesn't inspire confidence in your visitors that you're there for the long haul.
You can get hosting quite cheaply, about $4.00 per month for example, and you can get templates etc, from places like WordPress but I would strongly recommend paying a little more and getting all your website needs from somewhere like SBI (Solo Build It) or SiteBuilder.
When I started in 2006 I tried various ways to build my first site but it wasn't until I invested in SBI that I made any progress.
With the teaching and the action plan that comes with SBI you're way in front of the pack when it comes to building your site, that said, today I have sites built with both of these platforms.
You can investigate SBI here: http://bit.ly/2BSUTIO
You can investigate SiteBuilder here: http://bit.ly/2j4cvOC
The decision you will have to make is whether you wish to start a blog, and be prepared to commit to the regular creation of new content or a website and

have the unlimited possibilities which come with that.

OK, so you've made a decision on whether to go with a website or a blog, what next?

Well, next you've got to actually start building your eBusiness, read on.

BUILDING YOUR BUSINESS.

It's not my intention here to go into all the different aspects of building a website or a blog, suffice it to say that if you haven't done so already you'll need to find some help with things like search engine optimisation (SEO), keywords and the like, and there are more than enough good books and websites to help you with that, here I'm more interested in helping you to become a successful affiliate marketer once you've established a web presence be it small, as most of us start, or bigger if you already have a website/blog up and running.
A good place to start when it comes to building your business is to realise that it is actually a business that you're building and as such you're going to need to cultivate an audience who will eventually become your customers or clients.
Think of the places where you go to purchase whatever it is you need and then think of the reasons that you go to that particular store or supplier.
Most likely there will be several suppliers in your local area from whom you could make your purchase, why do you choose this one over that one?

Is it because they're the closest, they have the most knowledgeable or the friendliest staff, perhaps it's because their products are slightly better or a little cheaper than their competition, there's always a reason why people prefer one supplier to another, the next thing on your to do list is to find out what that reason is for those in your own marketplace.

Develop A Rapport.

As with a bricks and mortar business you'll need to convince potential buyers to come to you instead of going across the road and one very good way to do that is to establish yourself as an expert in your field.
If you're operating a grocery store with several hundred products to sell no one expects you to know everything about each product but as an affiliate you'll need to become the expert people come to when they need answers before they buy.
Developing a rapport with your audience and solving the problems that irk them the most will put you in good stead when they need to purchase something, after all if you can help someone when there's nothing in it for you you're a "good guy" and everyone likes to deal with a good guy, right?
In other words build a relationship first and ask for the money later.

Find Quality Products.

The next thing you need to do is to find a line of quality products or even just one or two quality products that you intend to promote.
More on this a little later but it is vitally important that the offerings you make to your audience are worthy of the time they spend investigating them and the money they will eventually pay for them.
Choose your products carefully, this is especially important as you're starting out, pick products that you would recommend to your family and friends, products that you can believe in and products that you have personal experience with if that's possible.
Promoting quality products will serve a twofold purpose, your customers will be happy to have dealt with you and it will also establish your brand as one which is reliable and trustworthy and this something which no amount of advertising can buy.

Establish Your Presence.

Next you have to start to establish yourself as an expert in your field and at the same time establish your brand.
(your brand is how you'll be recognised, just like Walmart, Toyota, Harley Davidson etc..)
There are a number of ways you can do that and several different options for the promotion of your brand, some of which I've outlined below.
1.   Connect with relevant influencers.
An influencer is an individual who holds the power to impact the purchasing decisions of a large segment of the population.
This person is in a great position to benefit from affiliate marketing.
They already boast an impressive following, so it's easy for them to direct consumers to the seller's products through social media posts, blogs, and other interactions with their followers.
The influencers would generally then receive a share of the profits they helped to create.
2.   Connect with relevant bloggers.
With the ability to rank organically in search engine queries, bloggers excel at increasing a seller's conversions.
The blogger samples the product or service and then writes a comprehensive review that promotes the brand in a compelling way, driving traffic back to the seller's site.
The blogger is rewarded in some way for his or her spreading the word about the value of the product, helping to improve the seller's sales.
3.   Become a recognised expert in your field.
How do you become a recognised expert?
You do things like write articles, you join relevant forums and be active, with no sales pitch, you answer questions on Q&A sites like Quora, you use your social media accounts to solve problems for others, in fact you do anything which will make life easier for those you want as potential customers.
4.   Build an email list.
Email lists are still the very best source of affiliate marketing income.
You will no doubt have heard the expression "the money's in the list" and this is so very true.

As your email list grows you have the ability to place your offering in front of more and more people.

These people are already warm prospects because they like what you're saying in your emails, if they didn't they wouldn't stay on your list.

You know that from personal experience, like me you will have unsubscribed from more email lists than you care to remember, only staying, and opening, those that offer you something of interest.

But be careful with your list, don't only mail them when you have something to sell, it's important that you offer something of value, something that will solve a problem for them or something that will answer a burning question they have, without the sales pitch every time.

No-one likes to be sold, people like to buy, it needs to be their decision and that will only happen when they like you and they like what you have to say when you're not trying to sell something.

A good rule of thumb that works for me is just one sales email per week at most and never two back to back.

Remember people buy from those they trust and those they like, cultivate those two things and you're on your way.

The next thing you must do of course is get people to visit your blog or website, how do you do that?

Read on!

Get Some Traffic!

Regardless of whether your intended destination for traffic is a sales page, a lead page, or simply a piece of content, the potential internet marketing methods are manifold.
We'll cover the most common ones here.

Email Marketing.

Email marketing is unique in this list for a very obvious reason: you already have their email address.

In other words, the main goal of email marketing is sales, whereas the other methods in this list can have both sales and lead generation as a goal.

Email marketing basically consists of sending promotional email messages to a list of leads, typically using an autoresponder service like GetResponse or Aweber.

Email marketing can be done on a completely manual basis, in which a business sends out newsletters or offers at their respective times, or on an automatic basis, in which a list of leads are put through a sequence of pre-planned auto-responder messages.

More recently, the concept of marketing automation has become popular.

This is where leads are put through a unique series of autoresponder sequences that change and adapt based on the actions of the lead and various "if this then that" (IFTTT) conditions established by the marketer.

For example, if a lead does not open an email, they might be automatically sent a follow-up email asking why they hadn't opened the previous one, or if a lead clicks on a certain link in an email which indicates they have a particular interest, they might be segmented into a separate list or new sequence that caters to that specific interest.

SEM or Search Engine Marketing.

Search Engine Marketing consists of leveraging a search engine's paid advertising platform to position your business as a "sponsored" search result in a prominent, visible place on Search Engine Results Pages (SERPs).

The most popular search engines for SEM at the moment are Google and Bing.

A business can setup their ad to target a group of keywords that they'd like to "rank" for, as well as selecting other variables such as demographics and location.

These ads will then appear at the top or bottom of the SERPs (depending on various factors such as budget and bidding) and will have the appearance of a typical search result, with the one exception of a small word like "ad" or "sponsored" somewhere on it (this varies among search engines).

SEO or Search Engine Optimization.
Search Engine Optimization is the use of various on-site and off-site practices and factors to make your web properties rank higher in search results.
These practices include methods like keyword usage, original content, frequent updating/posting, backlinking, social sharing, bounce rates (how many people leave after viewing just one page), visitors' average time on site, and the use of images and videos.
Until around 2012, SEO was arguably considered the most vital internet marketing method around and, depending on your industry, it might still be.
However, in recent years the growing number of competing web properties in the online space have made ranking very difficult and expensive for many businesses.
This, along with constant changes to some of the top search engines' algorithms have led many businesses to conclude that paid SEM is more cost-effective than SEO.
SEO still maintains its importance in many cases, however, such as in the case of local "brick and mortar" businesses whose search rankings are positively affected by the use of nearby city names in the search terms as well as the various search engines' use of locational data.

Ad Networks.
Ad networks are an excellent way to get your brand or offer in front of your target audience on a broad range of web properties.
The most commonly discussed ad network is Google's AdWords network but there are several other out there.

Using these networks will allow you to place banner image ads, video ads, or simple textual ads in front of web traffic on a variety of websites.
This approach can be especially powerful when combined with retargeting.
This entails placing retargeting pixels on your web properties and then specifically targeting your site visitors via ad networks so that the offer they initially looked at (and are presumably interested in) starts following them around the internet wherever they go.
This may sound creepy, but statistics indicate that people who are retargeted are 70% more likely to convert!

Individual Sites.
Some marketers might prefer to do their advertising on a case-by-case basis by personally approaching individual, relevant websites, forums, or blogs in their niche or industry.
When using this manual method, marketers should be sure to research the metrics of the given site, blog, or forum.
Naturally you'll want to display your ad in places with a reasonable level of traffic and a positive reputation to ensure your advertising dollars are spent well.
You can learn a lot about websites by researching them on Alexa.
That said, the majority of businesses tend to find the use of ad networks to be a more cost-effective way of advertising.

Social Media Marketing.
Social media marketing has come a long way in the last several years and has changed the way many businesses think about marketing in general.
For some marketers, social followers have replaced email addresses, posts and tweets have replaced promotional emails, and likes have replaced email opens.

Virtually every successful business today has not only a social media presence, but a clearly defined social media strategy.
Most of these strategies revolve around posting consistent content.
But it's more than just posting promotions and offers.
A successful social strategy will include various types of non-promotional content for various types of goals.
Posting about a charitable cause associates your brand with feelings of goodwill.
Posting about trendy topics makes your brand seem relevant.
Posting useful tips without a sales pitch makes your business come off as genuinely helpful.
Posting humorous or "feel-good" content associates your business with positive emotions, and so on.
But more importantly, these types of non-promotional posts are accomplishing two other goals.
First, they're encouraging social sharing, which grows your following even more.
Secondly, they're creating top-of-mind awareness for your brand.
People will get used to seeing your content and your business name, logo, and USP (Unique Selling Proposition).
As a result, when they have a problem that your business fixes, they'll be more likely to think of you first.
All of those social media concepts revolve around organic activity.
However, the major social media platforms today have also developed robust paid advertising systems.
The most game-changing of these has been the concept of social "native advertising".
Native advertising.
 Native advertising refers to advertisements that have the appearance of organic content with the exception of a tiny one-word disclaimer somewhere designating it as "sponsored" or an "advertisement".
This new form of paid social media advertising has proven to be remarkably effective because social media consumers are already in the habit of looking

at, consuming, and engaging with anything that looks like an organic post in their social feeds.
In addition to this, the line between organic posts and paid native ads have become increasingly blurred as these native ads act and function just like organic content (they can be shared, liked, etc.) and businesses now have the ability to pay to promote an organic post to give it further reach.

Video Marketing.
If there's one thing that has been well established in marketing today, it's the tremendous power of video.
Nothing else compares. Understandably then, marketers have seized on video and are leveraging it in numerous ways.
Video marketing is often executed as social media marketing.
Businesses are publishing video content on multiple video sites such as YouTube, DailyMotion, and Vimeo just as they would publish non-video content to Facebook or Twitter.
As with the social media strategy described earlier, a successful video content strategy includes a good mix of useful, helpful, trending, humorous, and "feel-good" video content, with "salesy" videos being in the minority.
Once published, video content should be cross-promoted on other social media platforms to increase exposure.
Another recent development is that major social networks like Facebook and Twitter have added their own video uploading and streaming functions, increasing the overlap between video marketing and social media marketing.
One further angle on video marketing is paid video advertising.
Presently, the most popular version of this is YouTube/AdWords video ads which appear at the beginning of videos on both YouTube as well as other video-playing properties around the web.
These video ads can typically be skipped after several seconds.
In addition to the YouTube/AdWords video ad network, businesses also often pay for video ads on an

individual basis on other websites, news sites, and so on.

Content Marketing.
Content marketing is largely included in the other marketing methods mentioned thus far, but it's also worth discussing by itself.
The most common forms of content marketing are blog posts, news articles, and social posting, but content marketing can also include video and image publishing.
The goals of content marketing are manifold.
Firstly, it builds goodwill with followers who associate your brand with helpful content.
Secondly, content marketing provides an opportunity to hide a "soft pitch" within "non-salesy" content which can lead to sales while at the same time providing useful content.
Thirdly, content marketing can be an excellent way to "pixel" an audience for later retargeting which has proven to be a devastatingly effective tactic.
Finally, content is the primary driver in most search engines' algorithms which can result in higher rankings.
There are many benefits beyond these four, but these can be considered the most relevant and directly impactful ones.

Old School Methods.
The following methods have largely become less common, if not altogether abandoned, because of negative connotations or even penalties that have been attached to them in the past.
But since it's theoretically possible to engage in these in a non-spammy manner, it's worth mentioning them briefly.
Blog commenting and video commenting can often be an effective way to get your brand in front of relevant audiences.
Just make sure that your comments are relevant, useful, and not spammy and definitely do not mass-

post comments for the sake of backlinking as that will likely kill your SEO thanks to recent search engine algorithms designed to penalize abusers of this tactic.

Forum posting is another marketing method that has become less popular today.

However, this was less due to abuses (although there certainly were some) and more towards a drifting away towards social media platforms.

It simply become more cost-effective and fruitful to focus on social media.

However, it is often the case that most of the serious devotees of a certain niche may be more likely to be found on niche-related forums, which means it can still be beneficial to market your brand in the signature section of your posts and interact on relevant forums periodically.

Just make sure you're making genuine and sincere contributions to the conversation.

There you have it, an (almost) complete guide to getting visitors to your blog or website, the important thing here is that all of these methods work if you implement them!

You have to take some action or none of the above will bring you visitors.

As you're relatively new to all of this I would suggest you concentrate on just one or perhaps two of these traffic getting methods until you're comfortable with them, to try to implement them all at once is just asking to become bogged down and that will eventually cause you to fail.

CONCLUSION.

That's it, there is nothing more you need to know to begin your new life as an affiliate marketer, as I said up front, quite simple really, except, well, it's not quite that simple, you still have to do the work, you have to remain positive and upbeat when things don't appear to be going as you'd like or as fast as you'd like and you have to persist, Rome wasn't built in a day and neither will your new lifestyle but, and remember this, Rome did eventually get built and look at it now!

As I said at the beginning I'd written about 15 pages of this little book when I sat down and thought "why am I bothering? There are 100s of books about affiliate marketing, many of them much more informative than this, why would anyone want this book?"
And then I remembered, when I first started affiliate marketing back in 2006 there was very little information that I could get free that would tell me the whole story.
All would offer some information and then ask for a subscription or try to sell an expensive course for me to get the real info that I needed.
It was really frustrating then and nothing much has changed.
You'll still get enough info to whet your appetite and then you'll be asked to part with sometimes quite large amounts of cash to learn how to make the whole thing work.
Not here.
There's no upsell, no course to buy, no membership to join, with this little book you get everything you need to know to get started on what may be the most exciting, and financially rewarding journey of your life.
Enjoy,
John.

MY RECOMMENDED RESOURCES.

For your website: (both include domain name registration & hosting, no more to pay)
Solo Build It (my personal recommendation)   -   http://bit.ly/2BSUTIO
SiteBuilder (also very good)   -   http://bit.ly/2j4cvOC

For your domain name: (if you need it)
GoDaddy   -
Namecheap   -

For your blog:

Wordpress -
Blogger -

For your site/blog hosting:
Bluehost -
Hostgator -

For your eMail:
Mailchimp -
AWeber -

For your niche products:
Clickbank -
Amazon -
C J Affiliate -
JVZoo -

If you've enjoyed this little book, if it's helped you or inspired you to start your affiliate marketing journey or perhaps you really think it's been a waste of your time, I'd like to know, please send me a note with your thoughts to jshaw2017@outlook.com

Thanks,
John.

Post Script.

If you need a more in depth guide I recommend "The Super Affiliate Handbook" by Rosalind Gardner, It's the amazing true story of a woman who, with NO business experience became a Super Affiliate earning $500,000+ per year selling other people's stuff online.
it's worth the money.

www.ingramcontent.com/pod-product-compliance
Lightning Source LLC
Chambersburg PA
CBHW031515210526
45464CB00007B/2915